THE MASTER
KEY TO RICHES

THE MASTER KEY TO RICHES

by Napoleon Hill

*The Secrets to Wealth,
Power, and Achievement
from the Author of*
Think and Grow Rich

Abridged and Introduced
by Mitch Horowitz

THE CONDENSED 📖 CLASSICS LIBRARY™

Published by Gildan Media LLC
aka G&D Media.
www.GandDmedia.com

The Master Key to Riches was originally published in 1945
G&D Media Condensed Classics edition published 2018
Abridgement and Introduction copyright © 2018 by Mitch
Horowitz

FIRST EDITION: 2018

Cover design by David Rheinhardt of Pyrographx

Interior design by Meghan Day Healey of Story Horse, LLC.

ISBN: 978-1-7225-0063-4

Contents

The Secrets to Power

This is probably the most unusual book Napoleon Hill ever wrote. He dramatically presents its text as a speech delivered by a "masked rich man," who decides to share his wealth secrets with the world. In using this device, Hill was borrowing a theme that has long been popular in America's alternative spiritual culture—placing lessons in the mouth of a mysterious master, who may be real, invented, or a mixture of both.

Hill's unknown speaker is basically a personification of the voice of practical wisdom that ran through all of his books. In *The Master Key to Riches*, the speaker captures the essentials of Hill's ideas and adds some additional insights that came to Hill when he published this book in 1945, toward the victorious end of World War II, with America's Great Depression finally a memory and his classic work, *Think and Grow Rich*, eight years behind him.

As with all of Hill's books, you can more or less glean the totality of his philosophy from this one, in which he states his seventeen principles of success, along with other lists and testaments that guide you through towards effectiveness, attainment, and achievement. *The Master Key to Riches* is notable in that it probably features more lists and bulleted points than ever before, and in a pleasingly compressed form so that the book serves as an introduction to the newcomer and a refresher to the veteran. In my view, a reader always benefits from a review of Hill's ideas, as each reading reveals something new or previously overlooked. That has been my personal experience.

Another important aspect of this book is that it features what I consider Hill's clearest and most sustained explanation of the power of the "applied faith." I have sometimes struggled with the idea of faith in Hill's program. Chapter eight, "Applied Faith," has proven especially helpful to me in that regard, and I direct you to pay close attention to it.

I now turn you over to the voice of Hill's "Masked Rich Man from Happy Valley," whose revelations and insights are the closest thing we have, and likely ever will, to a science of success.

—Mitch Horowitz

Think!

Many centuries ago a very wealthy and wise philosopher by the name of Croesus, an adviser to Cyrus, King of the Persians, said:

> *I am reminded, O King: and take this lesson to heart; that there is a Wheel on which the affairs of men revolve, and its mechanism is such that it prevents any man from being always fortunate.*

The Master Key to Riches was designed for the purpose of aiding men in the mastery and control of this great Wheel, to the end that it may be made to yield them an abundance of all that they desire, including the Twelve Great Riches of Life described in the second chapter.

Remember, you who are beginning the study of this philosophy, that this same Wheel that "prevents any man from being always fortunate" may provide also that no man shall be always unfortunate, provided he will take possession of his own mind and direct it to the attain of some Definite Major Purpose in life.

CHAPTER ONE

The Beginning of All Riches

The largest audience ever assembled in the history of mankind sat breathlessly awaiting the message of a mysterious man who was about to reveal to the world the secret of his riches.

Slowly the curtain began to rise. The speaker walked briskly to the podium. He was dressed in a long black robe and wore a mask over his eyes. His hair was grayish, and he appeared about sixty years of age.

He stood silently for a few moments, while the cameras flashed. Then, speaking slowly, in a voice soft and pleasing, like music, be began his message:

You have come here to seek the MASTER KEY TO RICHES!

You have come because of that human urge for the better things in life, which is the common desire of all people.

You desire economic security, which money alone can provide.

Some of you desire an outlet for your talents in order that you may have the joy of creating your own riches.

Some of you are seeking the easy way to riches, with the hope that you will find it without giving anything in return; that too is a common desire. But it is a desire I shall hope to modify for your benefit, as from experience I have learned that there is no such thing as something for noting.

There is but one sure way to riches, and it may be attained only by those who have the MASTER KEY TO RICHES!

The MASTER KEY is an ingenious device with which those who possess it may unlock the door to the solution all of their problems. Its powers of magic transcend those of the famous Aladdin's Lamp.

It opens the door to sound health.

It opens the door to love and romance.

It opens the door to friendship, by revealing the traits of personality and character that make enduring friends.

It reveals the method by which every adversity, every failure, every disappointment, every mistaken error of judgment, and every past defeat may be transmuted into riches of a priceless value.

It kindles anew the dead hopes of all who possess it, and it reveals the formula by which one may "tune in" and draw upon the great reservoir of Infinite Intelligence, through that state of mind known as Faith.

It opens the doors, one by one, to the Twelve Great Riches of Life, which I shall presently describe for you in detail.

Listen carefully to what I have to say, for I shall not pass this way again. Listen not only with open ears, but also with open minds and eager hearts, remembering that no man may hear that for which he has not the preparation for hearing.

Before I describe the Twelve Great Riches let me reveal to you some of the riches you already possess; riches of which most of you may not be conscious.

First, I would have you recognize that each of you is a plural personality, although you may regard yourself as a single personality. You and every other person consist of least two distinct personalities, and many of you possess more.

One is your "other self," a positive sort of person who thinks in terms of opulence, sound health, love and friendship, personal achievement, creative vision, service to others, and who guides you unerringly to the attainment of all of these blessings. It is this self which alone is capable of recognizing and approaching the

Twelve Great Riches. This is not an imaginary personality of which I speak. It is real.

When your negative personality is in control your radio station picks up only the negative thought vibrations that are being sent out by hundreds of millions of other negative personalities throughout the world. These are accepted, acted upon, and translated into their physical equivalent in terms of the circumstances of life that you do not wish.

When your positive personality is in control it picks up only the positive thought vibrations being released by millions of other positive personalities throughout the world, and translates them into their physical equivalent in terms of prosperity, sound health, love, hope, faith, peace of mind and happiness; the values of life for which you and every other normal person are searching.

I have come to reveal to you the Master Key by which you may attain these and many other riches. That mysterious key that unlocks the doors to the solution of all human problems, acquires all riches, and places every individual thought pattern under the control of one's "other self."

When I speak of "riches" I have in mind the greater riches whose possessors have made life pay off on their own terms—the terms of full and complete happiness. I call these the "Twelve Riches of Life." And I sincerely wish to share them with all of you who are prepared to receive them, in whole or in part.

You may wonder about my willingness to share, so I shall tell you that the MASTER KEY TO RICHES enables its possessors to add to their own store of riches everything of value when they share with others. This is one of the strangest facts of life, but it is a fact which each of you must recognize and respect. Now let us pass onto the description of the Twelve Riches.

CHAPTER TWO

The Twelve Riches of Life

*T**he greatest of all riches is . . .***

1. **A Positive Mental Attitude.** All riches of whatever nature, begin as a state of mind; and let us remember that a state of mind is the one and only thing over which any person has complete, unchallenged right of control. It is highly significant that the Creator provided man with control over nothing except the power to shape his own thoughts and the privilege of fitting them to any pattern of his choice. Mental attitude is important because it converts the brain into the equivalent of an electro-magnet, which attracts one's dominating thoughts, aims, and purposes. It also attracts one's fears, worries, and doubts. A positive mental atti-

tude is the starting point of all riches, whether they are riches of a material nature or intangible wishes. It attracts the wishes of a true friendship. And the riches one finds in the hope of future achievement.

2. **Sound Physical Health.** Sound health begins with a "health consciousness" produced by a mind that thinks in terms of health and not in terms of illness, plus temperance of habits in eating and properly balancing physical activities.

3. **Harmony in Human Relationships.** Harmony with others begins with one's self, for it is true, as Shakespeare said, and there are benefits available to those who comply with his admonitions, "To thine own self be true, and it must follow, as the night the day, thou cans't not then be false to any man."

4. **Freedom from Fear.** No man who fears anything is a free man! Fear is a harbinger of evil, and wherever it appears one may find a cause that must be eliminated before he may become rich in the fuller sense. The seven basic fears that appear most often in the mind of men are: (1) fear of POVERTY, (2) fear of CRITICISM, (3) fear of ILL HEALTH, (4) fear of LOSS OF LIFE, (5) fear of LOSS OF LIBERTY, (6) fear of OLD AGE, (7) fear of DEATH.

5. **The Hope of Achievement.** The greatest of all forms of happiness comes as a result of the hope

of achievement of some yet unattained desire; and poor beyond description is the person who cannot look to the future with hope that he will become the person he would like to be, or with the belief that he will attain the objective he has failed to reach in the past.

6. **The Capacity for Faith.** Faith is the connecting link between the conscious mind of the man and the great universal reservoir of Infinite Intelligence. It is the fertile soil of the garden of the human mind wherein may be produced all of the riches of life. It is the "eternal elixir" that gives creative power and action to the impulses of thought. Faith is the basis of so-called miracles, and of many mysteries that cannot be explained by the rules of logic or science. Faith is the "spiritual chemical" that, when it is mixed with prayer, gives one direct and immediate connection with Infinite Intelligence. Faith is the power that transmutes the ordinary energies of thought into their spiritual equivalent. And it is the one power through which the Cosmic Force of Infinite Intelligence may be appropriated to the uses of man.

7. **Willingness to Share One's Blessings.** He who has not learned the blessed art of sharing has not learned the true path to happiness, for happiness

comes only by sharing. And let it be forever remembered that all riches may be embellished and multiplied by the simple process of sharing them where they may serve others. And let it be also remembered that the space one occupies in the hearts of his fellowmen is determined precisely by the service he renders through some form of sharing his blessings.

8. **A Labor of Love.** There can be no richer man than he who has found a labor of love and who is busily engaged in performing it, for labor is the highest form of human expression of desire. Labor is the liaison between the demand and the supply of all human needs, the forerunner of all human progress, the medium by which the imagination of man is given the wings of action. And all labor of love is sanctified because it brings the joy of self-expression to him who performs it.

9. **An Open Mind on all Subjects.** Tolerance, which is among the higher attributes of culture, is expressed only by those who hold an open mind on all subjects at all times. And it is only the man with an open mind who becomes truly educated and who is thus prepared to avail himself of the greater riches of life.

10. **Self-discipline.** The man who is not master of

himself may never become the master of anything. He who is the master of self may become the master of his own earthly destiny, the "master of fate, the Captain of his soul." And the highest form of self-discipline consists in the expression of the humility of the heart when one has attained great riches or has been overtaken by that which is commonly called "success."

11. **The Capacity to Understand People.** The man who is rich in the understanding of people always recognizes that all people are fundamentally alike in that they have evolved from the same stem; that all human activities are inspired by one or more of the nine basic motives of life: (1) the emotion of LOVE, (2) the emotion of SEX, (3) the desire for MATERIAL GAIN, (4) the desire for SELF PRESERVATION (5) the desire for FREEDOM OF BODY AND MIND, (6) the desire for SELF-EXPRESSION, (7) the desire for perpetuation of LIFE AFTER DEATH, (8) the emotion of ANGER, and (9) the emotion of FEAR. And the man who would understand others must first understand himself.

12. **Economic Security.** The last, though not least in importance, is the tangible portion of the "Twelve Riches." Economic security is not attained by pos-

session of money alone. It is attained by the service one renders, for useful service may be converted into all forms of human needs, with or without the use of money.

Presently I shall acquaint you with the principles by which money and all other forms of riches may be obtained, but first you must be prepared to make application of these principles. Your mind must be conditioned for the acceptance of riches just as the soil of the earth must be prepared for the planting of seeds.

When one is ready for a thing it is sure to appear!

This does not mean the things one may need will appear without a cause, for there is a vast difference between one's "*needs*" and one's *readiness* to receive. To miss this distinction is to miss the major benefits I shall endeavor to convey. So let me lead you into *readiness* to receive the riches that you desire.

Chapter Three

The Eight Princes

My riches came through the aid of others. Some of these helpers have been well known. Some have been strangers whose names you will not recognize. Among these *strangers* are eight of my friends who have done most for me in preparing my mind for the acceptance of riches. I call them the "Eight Princes." They serve me when I am awake and they serve me when I am asleep.

The Princes serve me through a technique that is simple and adaptable. Every night, as the last order of the day's activities, the Princes and I have a roundtable session, the major purpose of which is to permit me to express my gratitude for the service they have rendered me during the day. My Princes of Guidance are:

1. PRINCE OF MATERIAL PROSPERITY, I am grateful to you for having kept my mind attuned to

the consciousness of opulence and plenty, and free from the fear of poverty and want.

2. PRINCE OF SOUND PHYSICAL HEALTH, I am grateful to you for having attuned my mind to the consciousness of sound health, thereby providing the means by which every cell of my body and every physical organ is being adequately supplied with an inflow of cosmic energy sufficient unto its needs, and providing a direct contact with Infinite Intelligence which is sufficient for the distribution and application of this energy where it is required.

3. PRINCE OF PEACE OF MIND, I am grateful to you for having kept my mind free from all inhibitions and self-imposed limitations, thereby providing my body and my mind with complete rest.

4. PRINCE OF HOPE, I am grateful to you for the fulfillment of today's desires, and for your promise of fulfillment of tomorrow's aims.

5. PRINCE OF FAITH, I am grateful to you for the guidance which you have given me; for your having inspired me to do that which has been helpful to me, and for turning me back from doing that which had it been done would have proven harmful to me. You have given power to my thoughts, momentum to my deeds, and the wisdom that has enabled me to understand the laws of Nature, and

the judgment to enable me to adapt myself to them in a spirit of harmony.

6. PRINCE OF LOVE, I am grateful to you for having inspired me to share my riches with all whom I have contacted this day; for having shown me that only that which I give away can I retain as my own. And I am grateful too for the consciousness of love with which you have endowed me, for it has made life sweet and all my relationships pleasant.

7. PRINCE OF ROMANCE, I am grateful to you for having inspired me with the spirit of youth despite the passing of the years.

8. PRINCE OF OVERALL WISDOM, my eternal gratitude to you for having transmuted into an enduring asset of priceless value, all of my past failures, defeats, errors of judgment and of deed, all fears, mistakes, disappointments, and adversities of every nature; the asset consisting of my willingness and ability to inspire others to take possession of their own minds and to use their mind-power for the attainment of the riches of life, thus providing me with the privilege of sharing all of my blessings with those who are ready to receive to them. And thereby enriching and multiplying my own blessings by the scope of their benefit to others.

Let me now share with you the following creed, so that you may adopt it as your own.

A HAPPY MAN'S CREED

I have found happiness by helping others to find it.

I have sound physical health because I live temperately in all things, and eat only the foods that Nature requires for body maintenance.

I am free from fear in all of its forms.

I hate no man, envy no man, but love all mankind.

I am engaged in a labor of love with which I mix play generously. Therefore I never grow tired.

I give thanks daily, not for more riches, but for wisdom with which to recognize, embrace, and properly use the great abundance of riches I now have at my command.

I speak no name save only to honor it.

I ask no favors of anyone except the privilege of sharing my riches with all who will receive them.

I am on good terms with my conscience. Therefore it guides me correctly in all that I do.

I have no enemies because I injure no man for any cause, but I benefit all with whom I come into contact by teaching the way to enduring riches.

I have more material wealth than I need because I am free from greed and covet only the material things I can use while I live.

I own the Estate of Happy Valley, which is not taxable because it exists mainly in my own mind in intangible riches, which cannot be assessed or appropriated except by those who adopt my way of life. I created this vast estate by observing Nature's laws and adapting my habits to conform therewith.

In the chapters that follow you fill find the MASTER KEY, which will unlock the door to this chamber and all others. And it will be in your hands when you have prepared yourself to accept it.

CHAPTER FOUR

Definiteness of Purpose

It is impressive to recognize that all of the great leaders, in all walks of life and during all periods of history, have attained their leadership by the application of their abilities to a *definite major purpose*.

It is no less impressive to observe that those who are classified as failures have no such purpose, but they go around and around, like a ship without a rudder, coming back always empty-handed, to their starting point.

Some of these "failures" begin with a definite major purpose but they desert that purpose the moment they are overtaken by temporary defeat or strenuous opposition. They give up and quit, not knowing that there is a philosophy of success which is as dependable and as definite as the rules of mathematics, and never suspecting that temporary defeat is but a test ground which may prove a blessing in disguise if it is not accepted as final.

It is one of the great tragedies of civilization that ninety-eight of out every one hundred persons go all the way through life without coming within sight of anything that even approximates definiteness of a major purpose!

We come now to the analysis of the power of definiteness of purpose, and psychological principles from which the power is derived.

FIRST PREMISE:

The starting point of all individual achievement is the adoption of a definite purpose and a definite plan for its attainment.

SECOND PREMISE:

All achievement is the result of a motive or combination of motives, of which there are nine basic motives, which govern all voluntary actions. (We described these nine motives in chapter two.)

THIRD PREMISE:

Any dominating idea, plan or purpose held in the mind, through repetition of thought, and emotionalized with a burning desire for its realization, is taken over by the subconscious section of the mind and acted upon, and it is thus carried through to its logical climax by whatever means may be available.

FOURTH PREMISE:

Any dominating desire, plan or purpose held in the conscious mind and backed by absolute faith in its realization, is taken over and acted upon immediately by the subconscious section of the mind, *and there is no known record of this kind of a desire having ever been without fulfillment.*

FIFTH PREMISE:

The power of thought is the only thing over which any person has complete, unquestionable control—a fact so astounding that it connotes a close relationship between the mind of man and the Universal Mind of Infinite Intelligence, the connecting link between the two being FAITH.

SIXTH PREMISE:

The subconscious portion of the mind is the doorway to Infinite Intelligence, and it responds to one's demands in exactly proportion to the quality of one's FAITH! The subconscious may mind be reached through faith and given instructions as though it were a person or a complete entity unto itself.

SEVENTH PREMISE:

A definite purpose, backed by absolute faith, is a form of wisdom, and wisdom in action produces results.

THE MAJOR ADVANTAGES OF DEFINITENESS OF PURPOSE

Definiteness of purpose develops self-reliance, personal initiative, imagination, enthusiasm, self-discipline, and concentration of effort, and all of these are prerequisites for the attainment of material success.

Definiteness of aim induces one to budget his time and to plan all his day-to-day endeavors so they lead toward the attainment of his MAJOR PURPOSE in life.

It makes one more alert in the recognition of opportunities related to the object of one's MAJOR PURPOSE, and it inspires the necessary courage to act upon those opportunities when they appear.

It inspires the cooperation of others.

It prepares the way for the full exercise of that state of mind known as FAITH, by *making the mind positive* and freeing it from the limitations of fear, doubt, and indecision.

It provides one with a *success consciousness*, without which no one may attain enduring success in any calling.

It destroys the destructive habit of procrastination.

Lastly, it leads directly to the development and the continuous maintenance of the first of the Twelve Riches, a *positive mental attitude*.

These are the major characteristics of DEFINITE-NESS OF PURPOSE, although it has many other qualities and usages, and it is directly related to each of the Twelve Riches because they are attainable only by singleness of purpose.

Definiteness of purpose can, and it should, so completely occupy the mind *that one has no time or space in the mind for thoughts of failure.*

CHAPTER FIVE

The Habit of Going the Extra Mile

An important principle of success in all walks of life and in all occupations is a willingness to GO THE EXTRA MILE; which means the rendering of more and better service than that for which one is paid, and giving it in a *positive mental attitude*.

Search wherever you will for a single sound argument against this principle, and you will not find it; nor will you find a single instance of enduring success that was not attained in part by its application.

The principle is not the creation of man. It is a part of Nature's handiwork, for its is obvious that every living creature below the intelligence of man is forced to apply the principle in order to survive.

Man may disregard the principle if he chooses, but he cannot do so and at the same time enjoy the fruits of enduring success.

Observe how Nature applies this principle in the production of food that grows from the soil, where the farmer is forced to GO THE EXTRA MILE by clearing the land, plowing it, and planting the seed at the right time of the year, for none of which he receives any pay in advance.

But, observe that if does his work in harmony with Nature's laws, and performs the necessary amounts of labor, Nature takes over the job where the farmer's labor ends, germinates the seed he plants, and develops it into a crop of food.

And, observe thoughtfully this significant fact: For every grain of wheat or corn he plants in the soil Nature yields him perhaps a hundred grains, thus enabling him to benefit by the law of increasing returns.

Nature GOES THE EXTRA MILE by producing enough of everything for her needs, together with a surplus for emergencies and waste; for example, the fruit on the trees, the bloom from which the fruit is grown, frogs in the pond and fish in the seas.

The advantages of the habit of GONG THE EXTRA MILE are definite and understandable. Let us examine some of them and be convinced:

The habit brings the individual to the *favorable attention* of those who can and will provide opportunities for self-advancement.

It tends to make one indispensable, in many different human relationships, and it therefore enables him to command more than average compensation for personal services.

It leads to mental growth and to physical skill and perfection in many forms of endeavor, thereby adding to one's earning capacity.

It enables one to profit by the law of contrast since *the majority of people do not practice the habit.*

It leads to the development of a positive, pleasing mental attitude, which is essential for enduring success.

It tends to develop a keen, alert imagination because it is a habit that inspires one continuously to seek new and better ways of rendering service.

It develops the important quality of personal initiative.

It develops self-reliance and courage.

It serves to build the confidence of others in one's integrity.

It aids the mastery of the destructive habit of procrastination.

It develops definiteness of purpose, ensuring one against the common habit of aimlessness.

There is still another, and a greater reason, for following the habit of GOING THE EXTRA MILE. *It gives one the only logical reason for asking for increased compensation.*

The attitude of the man who follows the habit of GOING THE EXTRA MILE is this: *He recognizes the truth that he is receiving pay for schooling himself for a better position and greater pay!*

This is an asset of which no worker can be cheated, no matter how selfish or greedy his immediate employer may be.

CHAPTER SIX

Love, the True Emancipator of Mankind!

L ove is man's greatest experience. It brings one into communication with Infinite Intelligence.

When it is blended with the emotions of sex and romance it may lead one to the higher mountain-peaks of individual achievement through *creative vision*.

The emotions of love, sex, and romance are the three sides of the eternal triangle of achievement known as genius. Nature creates geniuses through no other media.

Love is an outward expression of the spiritual nature of man.

Sex is purely biological, but it supplies the springs of action in all creative effort, from the humblest creation that crawls to the most profound of all creations, man.

When love and sex are combined with the spirit of romance the world may well rejoice, for these are the potentials of the great leaders who are the profound thinkers of the world.

The love of which I speak must not be confused with the emotions of sex, for love in its highest and purest expression is a combination of the eternal triangle, *yet it is greater than any one of its three component parts!*

The love to which I refer is the "élan vital"—the life-giving factor—the spring of action—of all creative endeavors that have lifted mankind to its present state of refinement and culture.

It is the one factor that draws a clear line of demarcation between man and all the creatures of the earth below him. It is the one factor that determines for every man the amount of space he shall occupy in the hearts of his fellowmen.

Love is the solid foundation upon which the first of the Twelve Riches may be built, *a positive mental attitude.* Love is the warp and woof of all the remaining eleven riches. It embellishes all riches and gives them the quality of endurance.

The *habit* of GOING THE EXTRA MILE leads to the attainment of that spirit of love, for there can be no greater expression of love than love that is demonstrated through service rendered completely and unselfishly.

The Master Mind

Definition: *An alliance of two or more minds, blended in a spirit of perfect harmony and cooperation for the attainment of a definite purpose.*

Note well the definition of this principle, for it carries a meaning that provides the key to the attainment of a great personal power.

The Master Mind is the basis of all great achievements, the foundation stone of major importance in all human progress, whether individual or collective.

The key to its power may be found in the word "harmony"!

Without that element, collective effort may constitute cooperation, but it will lack the power that harmony provides through coordination of effort.

The tenets of major importance in connection with the Master Mind are:

1. The Master Mind principle is the medium through which one may procure the full benefit of the *experience, training, education, specialized knowledge, and native ability of others*, just as completely as if their minds were one's own.

2. An alliance of two or more minds a spirit of *perfect* harmony for the attainment of a definite purpose, stimulates each individual mind with a high degree of inspiration, and may become that state of mind known as Faith! (A slight idea of this stimulation and its power is experienced in the relationship of close friendship and in the relationship of love.)

3. Every human brain is both a broadcasting and receiving station for the expression of the vibrations of thought, and the effect of the Master Mind principles stimulates action of thought, through what is commonly known as telepathy, operating through the sixth sense.

4. The Master Mind principle, when actively applied, has the effect of connection one with the subconscious section of the mind, and the subconscious sections of the minds of his allies—a fact that may explain many of the seemingly miraculous results obtained through the Master Mind.

5. The more important human relationships in connection with which one may apply the Master

Mind principle are: (a) marriage, (b) religion, and (c) in connection with one's occupation, profession, or calling.

The Master Mind principle made it possible for Thomas Edison to become a great inventor despite his lack of education and his lack of knowledge of the sciences with which he had to work—a circumstance that offers hope to all who erroneously believe themselves seriously handicapped by a lack of formal education.

There are two general types of Master Mind alliances:

1. Alliance, for purely personal reasons, with one's relatives, religious advisors and friends, where no material gain or objective is sought. *The most important of this type of alliance is that of man and wife.*
2. Alliances for business, professional, and economic advancement, consisting of individuals who have a personal motive in connection with the object of the alliance.

Never neglect forming a Master Mind alliance; great power can be attained in no other way.

Chapter Eight

Applied Faith

Faith is a royal visitor that enters only the mind that has been properly prepared for it; the mind that has been set in order through *self-discipline*.

In the fashion of all royalty, Faith commands the best room, nay, the finest suite, in the mental dwelling place.

It will not be shunted into servant's quarters, and it will not associate with envy, greed, superstition, hatred, revenge, vanity, doubt, worry, or fear.

Get the full significance of this truth and you will be on the way to an understanding of that mysterious power that has baffled scientists through the ages.

When the mind has been cleared of a *negative mental attitude*, the power of Faith moves in and begins to take possession!

Surely no student of this philosophy will be unfortunate enough to miss this important observation.

Let us turn now to analysis of Faith, although we must approach the subject with full recognition that Faith is a power that has defied analysis by the entire scientific world.

Faith is a state of mind that might properly be called the "mainspring of the soul" through which one's aims, desires, and purposes may be translated into their physical or financial equivalent.

Previously we observed that great power may be attained by the application of (1) the habit of GOING THE EXTRA MILE, (2) Definiteness of Purpose, and (3) the Master Mind. But that power is feeble in comparison with that which is available through the combined application of these principles with the state of mind known as Faith.

We have already observed that *capacity for faith* is one of the Twelve Riches. Let us now recognize the means by which this "capacity" may be filled with that strange power that has been the main bulwark of civilization, the chief cause of all human progress, the guiding spirit of all constructive human endeavor.

Let us remember that Faith is a state of mind that may be enjoyed only by those who have learned the art of taking *full and complete control* of their minds! This is the one and only prerogative right over which an individual has been given complete control.

Faith expresses its powers only through the mind that has been prepared for it. But the way of preparation is known, and may be attained by all who desire to find it.

The fundamentals of Faith are:

1. Definiteness of purpose supported by personal initiative or *action*.

2. The habit of GOING THE EXTRA MILE in all human relationships.

3. A Master Mind alliance with one or more people who radiate courage based on Faith, and who are suited spiritually and mentally to one's needs in carrying out a given purpose.

4. A positive mind, free from all negatives, such as fear, envy, greed, hatred, jealousy, and superstition. (A positive mental attitude is the first and the most important of the Twelve Riches.)

5. Recognition of the truth that every adversity carries with it the seed of equivalent benefit; that *temporary defeat is not failure* until it has been accepted as such.

6. The habit of affirming one's Definite Major Purpose in life in a ceremony of meditation at least once daily.

7. Recognition of the existence of Infinite Intelligence, which gives orderliness to the universe; that all individuals are minute expressions of this In-

telligence; and as such the individual mind has no limitations except those that are accepted and set up by the individual in his own mind.

8. A careful inventory (in retrospect) of one's past defeats and adversities, which will reveal the truth that all such experiences carry the seed of an equivalent benefit.

9. Self-respect expressed through harmony with one's own conscience.

These are the fundamentals of major importance that prepare the mind for the expression of Faith. Their application calls for no degree of superiority, but application does call for intelligence and *a keen thirst for truth and justice*.

Remember: faith fraternizes only with the mind that is positive!

How to Demonstrate the Power of Faith

1. Know what you want and determine what you have to give in return for it.

2. When you affirm the objects of your desires, through prayer, inspire your imagination to see

yourself already in possession of them, and act precisely as if you were in the physical possession thereof. (Remember the possession of anything first takes place mentally.)

3. Keep the mind open at all times for *guidance from within,* and when you are inspired by hunches to modify your plans or to move on a new plan, move without hesitancy or doubt.

4. When overtaken by temporary defeat, as you may be overtaken many times, remember that man's Faith is tested in many ways, and your defeat may be only one of your "testing periods." Therefore, accept defeat as an inspiration to greater effort, and carry on with belief that you will succeed.

5. Any negative state of mind will destroy the capacity for Faith and result in a negative climax of any affirmation you may express. Your state of mind is everything; therefore take possession of your mind and clear it completely of all unwanted interlopers that are unfriendly to Faith, and keep it cleared, no matter what may be the cost in effort.

6. Learn to give expression to your power of Faith by writing out a clear description of your Definite Major Purpose in life and using it as the basis of your daily meditation.

7. Associate with your Definite Major Purpose as many as possible of the nine basic motives, described previously.

8. Write out a list of all the benefits and advantages you expect to derive from the attainment of the object of your Definite Major Purpose, and call these into your mind many times daily, thereby making your mind "success conscious." (This is commonly called autosuggestion.)

9. Associate yourself, as far as possible, with people who are in sympathy with your Definite Major Purpose; people who are in harmony with you, and inspire them to encourage you in every way possible.

10. Let not a single day pass without making at least one definite move toward the attainment of your Definite Major Purpose. Remember, "Faith without works is dead."

11. Choose some prosperous person of self-reliance and courage as your "pacemaker," and make up your mind not only to keep up with that person, but to excel him. Do this silently, without mentioning your plan to anyone. (Boastfulness will be fatal to your success, as Faith has nothing in common with vanity or self-love.)

12. Surround yourself with books, pictures, wall mottoes, and other suggestive reminders of self-reliance founded upon Faith as it has been demonstrated by other people, thus building around yourself an atmosphere of prosperity and achievement. This habit will be fruitful of stupendous results.

13. Adopt a policy of never evading or running away from unpleasant circumstances, but recognize such circumstances and build a counter-fire against them right where they overtake you. You will discover that recognition of such circumstances, without fear of their consequence, is nine-tenths of the battle in mastering them.

14. Recognize the truth that everything worth having has a definite price. The price of Faith, among other things, is eternal vigilance in carrying out these simple instructions. Your watchword must be PERSISTENCE!

These are the steps that lead to the development and maintenance of a *positive mental attitude*, the only one in which Faith will abide. They are steps that lead to riches of both mind and spirit as well as riches of the purse. Fill your mind with this kind of mental food.

CHAPTER NINE

The Law of Cosmic Habitforce

We now come to the analysis of the greatest of all of Nature's laws, the law of Cosmic Habitforce!

Briefly described, the law of Cosmic Habitforce is Nature's method of giving fixation to all habits so that they may carry on automatically once they have been set into motion—the habits of men the same as the habits of the universe.

Every man is where he is and what he is because of his established habits of thought and deed. The purpose of this entire philosophy is to aid the individual in the formation of the kind of habits that will transfer him from where he is to where wishes to be.

Every scientist, and many laymen, know that Nature maintains a perfect balance between all the elements of matter and energy throughout the universe; that the entire universe is operated through an inexorable system of orderliness and habits that never vary, and cannot be altered by any form of human endeavor; that the five known realities of the universe are: (1) Time, (2) Space, (3) Energy, (4) Matter, and (5) Intelligence; these shaped the other known realities into orderliness and system based upon *fixed habits.*

These are nature's building-blocks with which she creates a grain of sand or the largest stars that float through space, and every other thing known to man, or that the mind of man can conceive.

These are the known realities, but not everyone has taken the time or the interest to ascertain that Cosmic Habitforce is the particular application of Energy with which Nature maintains the relationship between the atoms of matter, the stars and the planets in their ceaseless motion onward toward some unknown destiny, the seasons of the year, night and day, sickness and health, life and death. Cosmic Habitforce is the medium through which all habits and all human relationships are maintained in varying degrees of permanence, and the medium through which thought is translated into its physical equivalent in response to the desires and purposes of the individual.

But these truths are capable of proof, and one may count that hour sacred during which he discovers the inescapable truth that man is only an instrument through which higher powers than his own are projecting themselves. This entire philosophy is designed to lead one to this important discovery, and to enable him to make use of the knowledge it reveals, *by placing himself in harmony with the unseen forces of the universe, which may carry him inevitably into the success side of the great River of Life.*

The hour of this discovery should bring him within easy reach of the Master Key to all Riches!

Cosmic Habitforce is Nature's Comptroller through which all other natural laws are coordinated, organized, and operated through orderliness and system. Therefore it is the greatest of all natural laws.

The law of Cosmic Habitforce is Nature's own creation. It is the one universal principle through which order and system and harmony are carried out in the entire operation of the universe, from the largest star that hangs in the heavens to the smallest atoms of matter.

It is a power that is equally available to the weak and the strong, the rich and poor, the sick and well. It provides the solution to all human problems.

The major purpose of the seventeen principles of this philosophy is that of aiding the individual to adapt himself to the power of Cosmic Habitforce by self-disciple in connection with the formation of his habits of thought.

Let us turn now to a brief review of these principles, so that we may understand their relationship to Cosmic Habitforce. Let us observe how these principles are so related that they blend together and form the Master Key that unlocks the doors to the solution of all problems.

The analysis begins with the first principle of the philosophy:

1. THE HABIT OF GOING THE EXTRA MILE. This principle is given first because it aids in conditioning the mind for the rendering of useful service. And this condition prepares the way for the second principle—

2. DEFINITENESS OF PURPOSE. With the aid of this principle one may give organized direction to the principle of Going the Extra Mile, and make sure that it leads in the direction of his major purpose and becomes cumulative in its effects. These two principles alone will take anyone far up the ladder of achievement, but those who are aiming for the higher goals of life will need much help on the way, and this help is available through the application of the third principle—

3. THE MASTER MIND. Through the application of this principle one begins to experience a new and greater sense of power which is not available to the

individual mind, as it bridges one's personal deficiencies and provides him, when necessary, with any portion of the combined knowledge of mankind, which has accumulated throughout the ages. But this sense of power will not be complete until one acquires of art of receiving guidance through the fourth principle—

4. APPLIED FAITH. Here an individual begins to tune in to the powers of Infinite Intelligence, which is a benefit that is available only to the person who has conditioned his mind to receive it. Here the individual begins to take full possession of his own mind by mastering all fears, worries, and doubts, by recognizing his oneness with the source of all power. These four principles have been rightly called the "Big Four" because they are capable of providing more power than the average man needs to carry him to great heights of personal achievement. But these are adequate only for the very few who have other needed qualities of success, such as those provided by the fifth principle.

5. PLEASING PERSONALITY. A pleasing personality enables a man to sell himself and his ideas to others. Hence, it is an essential for all who desire to become the guiding influence in a Master Mind alliance. But observe carefully how definitely the

four preceding principles tend to give one a pleasing personality. These five principles are capable of providing one with stupendous personal power, but not enough power to ensure him against defeat, for defeat is a circumstance that every man meets many times throughout his life; hence the necessity of understanding and applying the sixth principle—

6. HABIT OF LEARNING FROM DEFEAT. Notice that this principle begins with the word "habit," which means that it must be accepted and applied as a matter of habit, under all circumstances of defeat. In this principle may be found hope sufficient to inspire a man to make a fresh start when his plans go astray, as go astray they must at one time or another.

7. CREATIVE VISION. This principle enables one to look into the future and to judge it by a comparison with the past, and to build new and better plans for attaining his hopes and aims through the workshop of his imagination. And here, for the first time perhaps, a man may discover his sixth sense and begin to draw upon it for the knowledge which is not available through the organized sources of human experience and accumulated knowledge. But, in order to make sure that he puts this bene-

fit to practical use he must embrace and apply the eighth principle—

8. PERSONAL INITIATIVE. This is the principle that starts action and keeps it moving toward definite ends. It insures one against the destructive habits of procrastination, laziness, and indifference. An approximation of the importance of this principle may be had by recognizing that it is the "habit-producer" in connection with the seven preceding principles, for it is obvious that the application of no principle may become a *habit* expect by the application of personal initiative. The importance of this principle may be further evaluated by recognition of the fact that it is the sole means by which a man may exercise full and complete control over the only thing the Creator has given him to control, *the power of his own thoughts*. But personal initiative is sometimes misdirected. Therefore it needs supplemental guidance from the ninth principle—

9. ACCURATE THINKING. Accurate thinking not only insures against the misdirection of personal initiative, but it also insures against errors of judgment, guesswork, and premature decisions. It also protects one against the influence of his own undependable emotions by modifying them

through the power of reason. The individual who has mastered these nine principles will find himself in possession of tremendous power, but personal power may be, and often is, dangerous if it is not controlled and directed through application of the tenth principle—

10. SELF-DISCIPLINE. Self-discipline cannot be had for the mere asking. Nor can it be acquired quickly. It is the product of carefully established and carefully maintained habits, which in many instances can be acquired only by many years of painstaking effort. So we have come to the point at which the power of the will must be brought into action, *for self-discipline is solely a product of the will*. Numberless men have risen to great power by the application of the nine preceding principles only to meet with ultimate failure. Self-discipline must begin with the application of the eleventh principle—

11. CONCENTRATION OF ENDEAVOR. The power of concentration is also a product of the will. It is so closely related to self-discipline that the two have been called the twin brothers of this philosophy. Concentration saves one from the dissipation of his energies, and aids him in keeping his mind focused upon the object of his Definite Major Purpose until it has been taken over by the

subconscious section of the mind and there made ready for translation into its physical equivalent, through the law of Cosmic Habitforce. It is the camera's eye of the imagination through which the detailed outline of one's aims and purposes are recorded in the subconscious; hence it is indispensible. But even these powers are not sufficient for every circumstance; there are times when one must have the friendly cooperation of many people, such as customers, clients, or voters, all of which may be had through the application of the twelfth principle—

12. COOPERATION. Cooperation differs from the Master Mind principle in that it is a human relationship that is needed, and may be had, without a definite alliance with others based upon a complete fusion of the minds. Without cooperation of others one cannot attain success in the higher brackets of personal achievement, for cooperation is the means of major value by which one may extend the space he occupies in the minds of others, which is sometimes called goodwill. Cooperation is attained more freely and willingly by the application of the thirteenth principle—

13. ENTHUSIASM. Enthusiasm is a contagious state of mind that not only aids one in gaining the coop-

eration of others, but more importantly, it inspires the individual to draw upon and use the power of his own imagination. It inspires action also in the expression of personal initiative, and it leads to the habit of concentration of endeavor. Moreover, it is one of the qualities of major importance in a pleasing personality, and it makes easy the application of the principle of Going the Extra Mile. In addition to all these benefits, enthusiasm gives force and conviction to the spoken word. Enthusiasm is the product of *motive*, but it is difficult to maintain without the aid of the fourteenth principle—

14. THE HABIT OF HEALTH. Sound physical health provides a suitable housing place for the operation of the mind; hence it is an essential for enduring success, assuming that the word "success" shall embrace all of the requirements for happiness. Here again the word "habit" comes into prominence, for sound health begins with a "health consciousness" that can be developed only by the right habits of living. Sound health provides the basis for enthusiasm, and enthusiasm encourages sound health; so the two are like the hen and the egg: no one can determine which came into existence first, but everyone knows that both are essential for

the production of either. Health and enthusiasm are like that. Both are essential for human progress and happiness.

15. BUDGETING TIME AND MONEY. Nearly everyone wishes to spend time and money freely, but budget and conserve them—never! However, independence and freedom of body and mind, the two great desires of all mankind, cannot become enduring realities without the self-discipline of a strict budgeting system. Hence, this principle is an essential part of the philosophy of individual achievement.

16. THE GOLDEN RULE *APPLIED*. Note the emphasis on the word "applied." Belief in the soundness of the Golden Rule is not enough. To be of enduring benefit, and in order that it may serve as a safe guide in the use of personal power, it must be applied as a matter of habit, in all human relationships. Quite an order, this! But the benefits that are available through the application of this profound rule of human relations are worthy of the efforts necessary to develop it into a habit. The penalties for failure to live by this rule are too numerous to describe. Now we have attained the ultimate in personal power, and we have provided ourselves

with the necessary insurance against its misuse. What we need from here on out is the means by which this power may be made permanent during our entire lifetime. We shall climax this philosophy, therefore, with the only known principle by which we may attain this desired end—the seventeenth and last principle of this philosophy—

17. COSMIC HABITFORCE. *Cosmic Habitforce* is the principle by which all habits are fixed and made permanent in varying degrees. As stated, it is the comptrolling principle of the entire philosophy, into which the preceding sixteen principles blend and become a part. And it is the comptrolling principle of all natural laws of the universe. It is the principle that gives the *fixation of habit* in the application of the principles of this philosophy. Mere understanding of the sixteen preceding principles will not lead anyone to the attainment of personal power. The principles must be understood and applied as a matter of strict habit, and habit is the sole work of the law of Cosmic Habitforce. Cosmic Habitforce is synonymous with the great River of Life, for it consists of a negative and a positive potentiality, as do all forms of energy.

You now have at your command a *complete philosophy* of life that is sufficient for the solution of every individual problem. It is a philosophy of principles, some combination of which has been responsible for every individual success in every occupation or calling.

CHAPTER TEN

Self-Discipline

Self-discipline is one of the Twelve Riches, but it is much more; it is an important prerequisite for the attainment of all riches, including freedom of mind and body, power and fame, and all the material things that are called wealth.

It is the sole means by which one may focus the mind upon the objective of a Definite Major Purpose until the law of Cosmic Habitforce takes over the pattern of that purpose and begins to translate it into its material equivalent.

It is the key to the volitional *power of the will* and the *emotions of the heart*, for it is the means by which these two may be mastered and balanced, one against the other, and directed to definite ends in *accurate thinking*.

It is the directing force in the maintenance of a Definite Major Purpose.

Also it operates entirely through the functioning system of the mind. Therefore, let us examine this system so that we may understand the factors of which it consists.

THE TEN FACTORS OF THE "MECHANISM" OF THOUGHT

The mind operates through ten factors, some of which operate automatically, while others must be directed through voluntary effort. *Self-disciple is the sole means of this direction.*

The ten factors are:

1. INFINITE INTELLIGENCE. The source of all power of thought, which operates automatically, but it may be organized and directed to definite ends through DEFINITENESS OF PURPOSE. Infinite intelligence may be likened to a great reservoir of water that overflows continuously, its branches flowing in small streams in many directions, and giving life to all vegetation and all living things. That portion of the stream that gives life to man supplies him also with the power of thought.

2. THE CONSCIOUS MIND. The individual mind functions through two departments. One is known as the conscious section of the mind; the other the

subconscious. It is the opinion of psychologists that these two sections are comparable to an iceberg, the visible portion above the waterline representing the conscious section, and the invisible portion below the waterline representing the subconscious. Therefore it is obvious that the conscious section of the mind—that portion with which we consciously and voluntarily turn on the power of thought—is but a small portion of the whole, consisting of perhaps one-fifth of the available mind power. All the other essential functions are performed by the subconscious mind, which also serves as the connecting link between the conscious mind and *Infinite Intelligence.* It may be likened to the spigot of the consciousness mind, through which (by its control through self-discipline) more thought power may be turned on. Or it may be likened to a rich garden spot wherein may be planted and germinated the seed of any desired idea.

3. THE FACULTY OF WILLPOWER. The power of the will is the "boss" of all departments of the mind. It has the power to modify, change, or balance all thinking habits, and its decisions are final and irrevocable except by itself. It is the power that puts the emotions of the heart under control, and it is subject to direction only by self-discipline. In

this connection, it may be likened to the Chairman of the Board of Directors whose decisions are final. It takes its orders from the conscious mind, *but recognizes no other authority.*

4. THE FACULTY OF REASON. This is the "presiding judge" of the conscious section of the mind, which may pass judgment on all its ideas, plans, and desires, and it will do so if it is directed by self-discipline. But its decisions can be set aside by the power of the will, or modified by the power of the emotions when the will does not interfere. Let us here take note that all accurate thinking requires the cooperation of the faculty of reason, *although it is a requirement which not more than one person in every ten thousand respects.* This is why there are so few accurate thinkers. Most so-called thinking is the work of the emotions without the guiding influence of self-discipline; without relationship to either the power of the will or the faculty of reason.

5. THE FACULTY OF THE EMOTIONS. This is the source of most of the actions of the mind, the seat of most of the thoughts released by the conscious section of the mind. The emotions are tricky and undependable and may be very dangerous if they are not modified by the faculty of reason under the direction of the faculty of the will.

However, the faculty of the emotions is not to be condemned because of its unpredictability, for it is the source of all enthusiasm, imagination, and Creative Vision, and it may be directed by self-discipline to the development of these essentials of individual achievement. The direction may be given by modification of the emotions through the faculties of the will and the reason. *Accurate thinking* is not possible without complete mastery of the emotions. The emotions that are most important and most dangerous are: (1) the emotion of sex, (2) the emotion of love, and (3) the emotion of fear. *These are the emotions that produce the major portion of all human activities.* The emotions of love and sex are creative. When controlled and directed they inspire one with imagination and creative vision of stupendous proportions. If they are not controlled and directed they may lead one to indulge in tremendous follies.

6. THE FACULTY OF IMAGINATION. This is the workshop wherein are shaped and fashioned all desires, ideas, plans, and purposes, together with the means of attaining them. Through organized use and self-discipline the imagination may be developed to the status of Creative Vision. But the faculty of the imagination, like the faculty of the

emotions, is tricky and undependable if it is not controlled and directed by self-discipline. Without control it often dissipates the power of thought in useless, impractical, and destructive activities. *Uncontrolled imagination is the stuff that daydreams are made of!*

7. THE FACULTY OF CONSCIENCE. The conscience is the moral guide of the mind, and its major purpose is modifying the individual's aims and purposes so that they harmonize with the moral laws of nature and of mankind. The conscience is the twin-brother of the faculty of reason in that it gives discrimination and guidance to the reason when reason is in doubt. The conscience functions as a cooperative guide only so long as it is respected and followed. If it is neglected, or its mandates are rejected, it finally becomes a conspirator instead of a guide, and often volunteers to justify man's destructive habits. Thus the dual nature of the conscience makes it necessary for one to direct it through strict self-discipline.

8. THE SIXTH SENSE. This is the "broadcasting station" of the mind through which one automatically sends and receives the vibrations of thought commonly known as telepathy. It is the medium through which all thought impulses and hunches

are received. And it is closely related to, or perhaps it may be a part of, the subconscious. The sixth sense is the medium through which Creative Vision operates. It is the medium through which all basically new ideas are revealed. And it is the major asset of the minds of all who are known as geniuses.

9. THE MEMORY. This is the filing cabinet of the brain, wherein is stored all thought impulses, all experiences, and all sensations that reach the brain through the five physical senses.. And it may be the filing cabinet of all impulses of thought that reach the mind through the sixth sense. The memory is tricky and undependable unless it is organized and directed by self-discipline.

10. THE FIVE PHYSICAL SENSES. These are the physical arms of the brain through which it contacts the external world and acquires information. The physical senses are not reliable, and therefore require constant self-discipline. Under any kind of intense emotional activity the senses become confused and unreliable. The five senses are easily deceived. And they are deceived daily by the common experiences of life. Under the emotion of fear the physical senses often create monstrous "ghosts" that have no existence except in the faculty of the

imagination, and there is no fact of life that they will not exaggerate or distort when fear prevails. In this sense, fear is the archenemy of mankind.

Before leaving the analysis of self-discipline, which deals entirely with the mechanism of thought, let us briefly describe some of the known facts and habits of thought in order that we may acquire the art of accurate thinking.

1. All thought (whether it is positive or negative, good or bad, accurate or inaccurate) tends to clothe itself in its physical equivalent, and it does so by inspiring one with ideas, plans, and the means of attaining desired ends, through logical and natural methods.

2. Through the application of self-discipline thought can be influenced, controlled, and directed through transmutation to a desired end, by the development of voluntary habits suitable for the attainment of any given end.

3. The power of thought (through the aid of the subconscious) has control over every cell of the body and all the effects therein. These functions are carried on automatically but many may be stimulated by voluntary aid.

4. All of man's achievements begin in the form of thought, organized into plans, aims, and purposes, and expressed in terms of physical action. All action is inspired by one or more of the nine basic motives.

5. The entire power of the mind operates through the conscious and subconscious. The conscious section is under the control of the individual; the subconscious is controlled by Infinite Intelligence and is the medium of communication between Infinite Intelligence and the conscious mind.

6. Both the conscious and subconscious function in response to fixed habits, whether the habits are voluntary or involuntary.

7. The majority of one's thoughts are inaccurate because they are inspired by personal opinions that are reached without examination of the facts, or because of bias, prejudice, fear, and emotional excitement.

8. The first step in accurate thinking is that of separating facts from hearsay evidence and emotional reactions. The second step is that of separating facts, after they have been identified as such, into two classes: important and unimportant. An important fact can be used to help you attain your major purpose. All other facts are relatively unimportant.

9. Desire, based on a definite motive, is the beginning
   of all voluntary thought action associated with individual achievement. The presence in the mind of
   any intense desire tends to stimulate the faculty of
   the imagination with the purpose of creating ways
   and means of attaining the desire.

These are some of the more important of the known
facts concerning the greatest of mysteries, the mystery
of human thought, and they indicate clearly that accurate thinking is attainable only by the strictest habits of
self-discipline.

The lights were now dimmed. The masked rich man
from Happy Valley finished speaking and disappeared
into the darkness as mysteriously as he had arrived, but
he had given every member of that huge audience a new
birth of hope, faith, and courage.

*Remember it is profoundly significant that the only
thing over which you have complete control is your own
mental attitude!*

If the rich man from Happy Valley has brought you
nothing but this great truth he has provided you with
a source to riches of incomparable value; for this is the
Master Key to Riches!

NAPOLEON HILL was born in 1883 in Wise County, Virginia. He was employed as a secretary, a reporter for a local newspaper, the manager of a coalmine and a lumberyard, and attended law school, before he began working as a journalist for *Bob Taylor's Magazine,* an inspirational and general-interest journal. In 1908, the job led to his interviewing steel magnate Andrew Carnegie. The encounter, Hill said, changed the course of his life. Carnegie believed success could be distilled into principles that anyone could follow, and urged Hill to interview the greatest industrialists, financiers, and inventors of the era to discover these principles. Hill accepted the challenge, which lasted more than twenty years and formed the building block for *Think and Grow Rich.* Hill dedicated the rest of his life to documenting and refining the principles of success. After a long career as an author, magazine publisher, lecturer, and consultant to business leaders, the motivational pioneer died in 1970 in South Carolina.

MITCH HOROWITZ, who abridged and introduced this volume, is the PEN Award-winning author of books including *Occult America* and *The Miracle Club: How Thoughts Become Reality*. *The Washington Post* says Mitch "treats esoteric ideas and movements with an even-handed intellectual studiousness that is too often lost in today's raised-voice discussions." Follow him @MitchHorowitz.